D1472848

HOW TO BE...

an ARTIST

Stephanie Turnbull

A$^+$

Smart Apple Media

Published by Smart Apple Media, an imprint of Black Rabbit Books
P.O. Box 3263, Mankato, Minnesota, 56002
www.blackrabbitbooks.com

U.S. publication copyright © 2016 Smart Apple Media.
International copyright reserved in all countries.
No part of this book may be reproduced in any
form without written permission from the publisher.

Printed in the United States of America, at Corporate Graphics
in North Mankato, Minnesota

Designed and illustrated by Guy Callaby
Edited by Mary-Jane Wilkins

Cataloging-in-Publication Data is available from the Library of Congress

ISBN 978-1-62588-365-0

Photo acknowledgements
t = top, b = bottom, c = center, l = left, r = right
page 1 Serg_Velusceac; 3t Picsfive/both Thinkstock, l LEGEN -wait for
it- DARY, r chevanon, b Eric Boucher; 4 Jaimie Duplass; 5t alicedaniel/
all Shutterstock, b Diamantis Seitanidis/Thinkstock; 6 akekoksomshutter;
8t Eky Studio, b photka; 10 MarArt; 11 NEGOVURA; 12t Pefkos, l Radu
Bercan; 13l Perun, r Anna Sedneva/all Shutterstock, b photka/Thinkstock;
14t Madlen, l Elena Schweitzer, r Evgeny Tomeev, b V. J. Matthew/all
Shutterstock; 15 collage images from Shutterstock and Thinkstock; 18 (boy)
Gladskikh Tatiana, (image) Irina_QQQ; 19 ZouZou; 20 NJB Photography/all
Shutterstock; 21 HTuller/Thinkstock; 22 egluteskarota; 23 ConstantinosZ;
24 GOLFX/all Shutterstock
Cover Kuttelvaserova Stuchelova/Shutterstock

DAD0060
022015
9 8 7 6 5 4 3 2 1

Contents

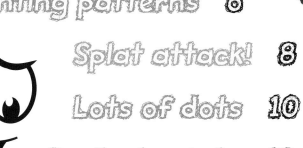

Starter skills

If you love to paint, draw, and be creative, try the arty techniques in this book. You'll soon be producing all kinds of amazing art—and who knows, one day you might be a famous artist!

HANDY HINTS

Look out for the thumbs up. Here you'll find tips to help you build on and improve your skills.

This warning hand is for important safety facts.

You may already have crayons, paper, brushes, and other useful art supplies.

Be organized

Find a suitable space to work in. Protect surfaces with newspaper, wear an apron or old clothes, and collect all your equipment before you begin. Don't rush your work, and always tidy up afterward.

Sticking cardboard cut-outs on a painted background gives a great 3D effect.

Experiment!

Some artists paint **watercolor** scenes or create vibrant portraits in **acrylics**. Others make **abstract** art with shapes and colors, or use **collage** for textured effects. Try lots of styles to discover which kind of art you like best!

Painting patterns

Start by having fun with **poster paints!** They're cheap, come in bottles or jars, and are great for covering large areas with bright colors.

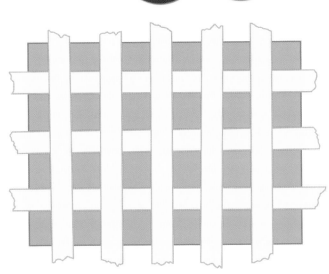

3D squares

1 Start with a large piece of colored card. Stick strips of masking tape across and down the card to make a criss-cross pattern.

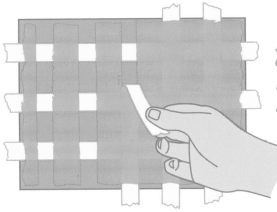

2 Now cover the card with paint. Leave to dry, then carefully peel off the tape strips.

3 Stick on a new set of strips. Make sure that they overlap the painted squares slightly. Choose or mix another color to paint on top.

 Use fat, wide brushes to cover the paper quickly.

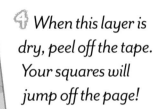

4 When this layer is dry, peel off the tape. Your squares will jump off the page!

Use the patterned paper to wrap a birthday present.

WHAT NEXT? Look at a color wheel: it shows the three **primary colors**—red, yellow, and blue—plus other colors you can make by mixing them. Choose similar colors to create shades and shadows, or pair a color with the one opposite to make both colors stand out.

Opposite colors are called complementary colors.

Primary colors

Splat attack!

Try painting without a brush. Some artists pour or drip paint, or even throw it at the canvas! Here are some messy ways of creating brilliantly bold art.

Use large sheets of paper and make sure the paint goes on them—not all over the room!

Blob monsters

1 Put some poster paint in a bowl and add a little water so it's runny.

2 Tip a few drops of paint on a sheet of paper. Carefully blow the paint outwards with a drinking straw to make shapes.

3 *Let the paint dry, then turn your splats into monsters by adding details with marker pen. Use your imagination to create all kinds of crazy creatures.*

WHAT NEXT? *Dip an old toothbrush in runny paint and scrape a piece of card across it (toward yourself) so the paint sprays over the paper.*

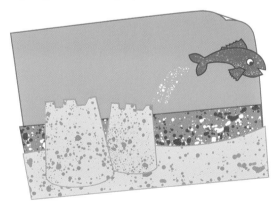

Experiment with different colors, leave to dry, then cut out shapes to make pictures. Try a seaside scene with speckled sandcastles and sparkling sea, or a starry night sky with planets.

Lots of dots

Another neat painting method involves using cotton buds or a thin, pointed brush to make tiny dots. This is called **pointillism** and creates eye-catching paintings.

1 *Find a magazine photo of a simple object, such as a piece of fruit. Carefully trace or copy the image with a pencil on thick paper.*

2 *Mark areas of different colors or shades.*

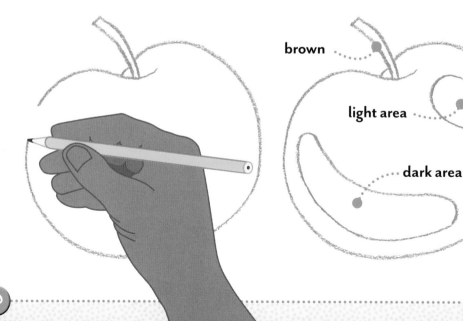

brown

light area

dark area

3 Start filling the shape with tiny paint dots. Try to make each dot the same size. For lighter places, place the dots farther apart. Put the dots closer together in the darker areas.

4 Leave your painting to dry, then rub out the pencil lines.

WHAT NEXT? Sketch a pattern, then go over it with dots. Start at the far side of the paper so you don't smudge the paint as you work.

Don't rush your dots or they'll look messy. The neater they are, the better the effect.

Build up detailed dotty patterns to create a fantastic **mosaic** *effect.*

Perfect prints

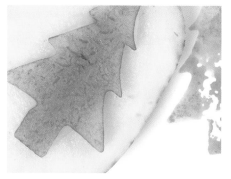

Make stylish designs by dipping small sponges or potato halves into paint and printing them on paper. Here are some more ideas.

Food prints

Lemons make fantastic printing tools! Cut one in half and dip it in paint. Test prints on scrap paper first as too much paint will just make a solid blob—you need to see the delicate patterns in the segments of fruit.

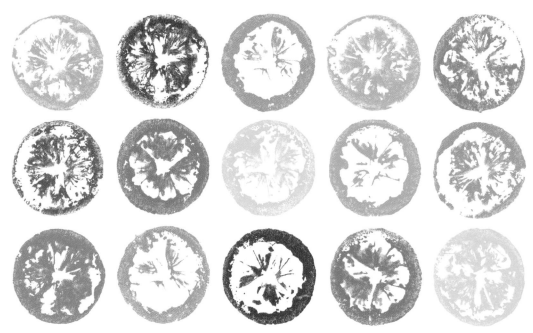

Body printing

Use your fingers, hands, or even feet to create personalized prints.

Try printing with other fruits and vegetables, such as halved apples or bell peppers. How about a star fruit?

Leave fingerprints to dry, then draw details to turn them into animals.

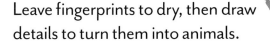

WHAT NEXT?

Hunt for objects with interesting shapes and textures. Try printing with bubble wrap, buttons, cookie cutters, or old shoes with patterned soles.

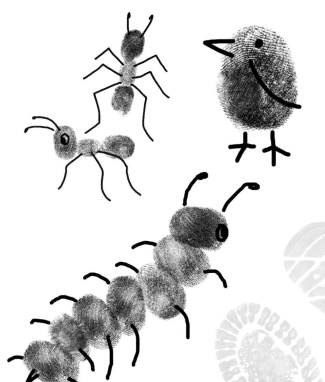

Clever collage

Get creative with collage!
Choose materials such as
fabric, pasta, sweets, or
shells and glue them in
a pattern on paper—or
use them to decorate
a photo frame.

Layered paper

Tissue paper is perfect for collages as
you can layer it to create different shades.

*1 Tear or cut long strips
of tissue paper to make a hilly
landscape or a beach scene.*

*2 Cut a few small details
and stick them on top.*

Fantastic photos

Make great photo collages using pictures cut from old magazines.
Put lots of images together to create weird and wonderful scenes...

... or make funny
faces using a jumble
of body parts!

*Start with large
background images,
then add lots of smaller
photos on top.*

*Try making
collage cards
for your
friends and family.*

Cool cartoons

Artists should never be without a pencil to doodle patterns, sketch ideas, or draw detailed pictures. Try these comic characters to see whether you could have a career as a cartoonist!

Funny faces

1 To draw a cartoon face, lightly sketch two ovals.

2 Add eyes, eyebrows, hair, a nose, mouth, ear, and neck.

3 Use your guidelines to draw the final face, using darker lines. Carefully erase any extra lines.

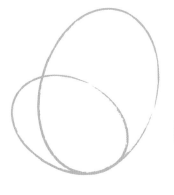

4 Draw this face a few times and experiment with expressions: draw the eyes closed and mouth open to show laughter, or the eyebrows low and mouth smaller to show grumpiness.

Soft pencils smudge easily, so don't rest your hand on your work and spoil your drawing.

WHAT NEXT?

Try sketching cartoon animals using simple shapes. Here are some dinosaur outlines to start with.

Add horns, spikes, or bony plates to invent your own amazing dinosaurs.

Computer art

Why not use a computer to create art? There are many programs that let you draw pictures or clever patterns.

Tessellations

Try making a **tessellation** using a program such as Microsoft Paint.

2 *Use the free-form select tool to cut a wiggly section from the bottom of the shape.*

1 *Select the solid rectangle tool and draw a rectangle or square. Fill it with color.*

Select the icon that makes the background see-through, or you won't be able to move the shape without a white section attached.

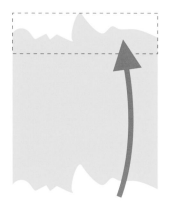

3 *Move the cut section to the top of the shape.*

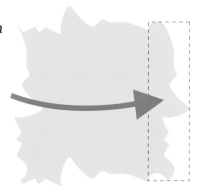

4 *Cut a section from the left of the shape and move it to the right.*

5 Go to the select tool (a dotted-line box) and draw a box around the shape. Copy and paste it, then change its color. Move it to line up with the first shape.

6 Add more shapes to fill the page.

Use your digital designs as wallpaper on your computer.

WHAT NEXT?
Scan photos and **crop** them to focus on interesting details, or turn them black and white for an arty effect.

Body art

Some artists paint hands, faces, or even whole bodies. Experiment with body art by painting your friends' faces. Always use proper **face paints** —ordinary paint damages skin.

*Test a small amount of face paint on the person's skin first to check they're not **allergic** to it. Never paint on sore or broken skin.*

*These amazing patterns are made using a reddish-brown dye called **henna**.*

Tiger face

Invent your own designs with flowers, swirls, and shapes, or try this tiger.

1 *Put yellow paint on a damp sponge and dab a thin layer over the middle of the face. Avoid eyes.*

2 *Sponge around the outside of the face with orange.*

3 Use a brush to paint white, spiky eyebrows, cheek stripes, and pointy whiskers around the mouth.

4 Paint the tip of the nose black and draw a line down to the top lip. Add black dots and whiskers around the mouth area. Paint black cheek stripes between the white ones.

WHAT NEXT?
Practice painting thin lines with a pointed brush to create detailed designs. Sprinkle on body glitter to make your art stand out even more.

Glossary

abstract
A piece of art that doesn't show people, places, or objects, but uses colors and shapes to suggest ideas or feelings.

acrylics
Bright, fast-drying paints usually sold in tubes. Acrylics don't wash off when dry, so don't get them on your clothes!

allergic
Having a bad reaction to something, for example a skin product, that can lead to a rash, swelling, or other problems.

collage
A collection of materials that have been arranged and glued to a surface.

collage

crop
To trim a picture with scissors or a cropping tool on a computer so that only the most important or impressive parts remain.

face paints
Paints designed to be used on skin and to wash off easily. Never use ordinary paints on your face, as the ingredients could make skin sore or itchy.

henna
A paste used to paint detailed patterns on skin, usually hands and feet. People in India and other Asian countries often wear henna to celebrate weddings and festivals.

mosaic
A design made up of lots of small pieces of colored glass, stone, or other materials.

pointillism
A type of painting in which patterns of dots create pictures. It was developed in the 1880s by two French artists, Georges Seurat and Paul Signac.

poster paints
Water-based paints that come in lots of bright colors. Poster paints are sometimes sold as powder to mix with water.

primary colors
A set of colors that can be combined to make lots of other colors.

tessellation
A flat covering made up of shapes that fit together without any gaps or overlaps.

watercolor
A type of paint that is mixed with water. Water-colors work best on paper, but you can try them on surfaces such as wood.

www.kinderart.com/painting
Find easy and effective ideas for creating a range of paintings.

www.how-to-draw-cartoons-online.com
Follow simple steps to draw all kinds of cartoons, including aliens, animals, dinosaurs, people, robots, and many more.

www.tessellations.org
Look at lots of amazing tessellations and learn how to make your own.

Index

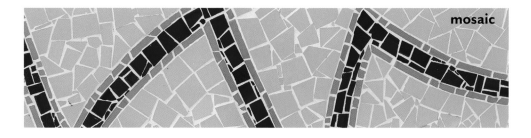

mosaic